Less Stressed More Blessed

Experience The Positive Changes In Your Life Through Relaxation And Stress Reduction

Table of Contents

Introduction

This book contains proven steps and strategies on how to manage your stress effectively and live a happier, more contented life.

Before you are introduced to easy-to-follow yet effective relaxation techniques, this book first deals with your biggest enemy – your mind. Stress is a ghost that hides inside your subconscious mind, so it is important to clear your headfirst and understand what stress is really all about.

Chapter 1: Balancing Stress And Relaxation

Do you know that stress can reduce your lifespan by several years? It deteriorates health by releasing harmful hormones in the body that consume the muscles, slow down metabolism, raise blood sugar and blood pressure, decrease energy production, render digestion less efficient, weaken the immune system, weaken the heart, and impair the brain. Recently, stress has also been linked to non-age related macular degeneration. In other words, stress causes you to be less efficient and functional.

Contrary to what many people believe, stress is not just in the mind but is also a physical phenomenon that manifests through tangible signs and symptoms. These signs and symptoms not only affect quality of life but can also change your life forever. Relationships get broken, careers lost, emotional stability lost – stress definitely alters the way you perceive happiness and feel comfort, so unless you do something about it, your life might not be as fulfilling as you want it to be.

Balancing stress and relaxation is very important for achieving well-being. Yet, why should you balance stress out instead of getting rid of it? As the title of the book implies – *Less Stressed* – the goal here is to lower stress while increasing relaxation because completely eliminating stress is quite impossible. It is everywhere, and whether you like it or not, it will always be a part of life. It can be your neighbor, the economy, the traffic, or even the weather.

Any of your coworkers and bosses might cause you stress at any moment. Traffic and road accidents might prevent you from observing punctuality all the time. Your dog might pee on your carpet, and you cannot do anything about it because you cannot control everything. Thus, from this moment forward, you have to accept the presence and dangers of stress.

Now you need to learn to balance stress and relaxation. There are two stages: reducing stress and inducing relaxation.

Reducing stress has three steps: acceptance, avoidance, and adaptation.

Acceptance

People fail to experience relaxation because they do not acknowledge the need for it. They cannot find a solution if they do not accept that there is a problem. If you are one of these people, you are denying reality, and living in denial does not lead to healthy living.

Maybe your job is too stressful to handle, and perhaps it is more practical to look for another job that is more fulfilling. Accept that you dislike your job and that adjustment is probably not an option. It might be out of your comfort zone, but this is essential for growth.

Maybe your marriage is no longer worth keeping because the love has faded. Accept that your marriage is drifting apart, and you have limited options for repairing it.

Maybe your neighbor's dogs are upsetting you. They bark so loud, you cannot find quiet time. Accept the fact that your neighbor is not moving out with the dogs, and the best option is to find an amicable compromise before filing a formal complaint.

By accepting that some stressors are out of your control and will always be there no matter what, you can recognize the stressors you can eliminate.

Avoidance

Once you have accepted that some stressors are there to stay, the next thing to do is avoid what you can. Because you have accepted their existence, you can now clearly see where the stressors are. Thus, you can anticipate them and avoid them completely.

In the process of avoidance, you also eliminate some stressors because they no longer get in your way. Stressors that do not bother you are stressors that no longer exist in your world. You also automatically make some adjustments to make handling things better, which is part of the third step.

The heavy traffic on the freeway is probably stressing you out every day because gridlock is common during rush hour. The only way to avoid this stressor is to use that road at a different time. Waking up earlier to avoid the traffic might be a source of stress at first, but as you adjust to it, you will realize that it is the smarter choice.

Your boss is probably giving you more tasks than you can handle, and the pile of paperwork and deadlines are already clouding your sound judgment. In this case, tell your boss how you feel, and reason out that the completion of some tasks is impossible.

That way, you can avoid unnecessary additional work.

Your coworker is probably driving you mad most of the time because he keeps on giving you wrong information and passing on his responsibilities to you. Tell him about the issue, and if he does not acknowledge the problem, voice it to your superiors, so you can avoid conflicts.

Avoidance is not always easy. As given in the examples above, avoidance sometimes entails drastic actions and responses that might make you uncomfortable at first. Nonetheless, the changes they bring are more than pleasing and fulfilling.

Adaptation

For the stressors you have accepted but cannot avoid, the only option left is adaptation. Since they will be in your life whether you like it or not, the best thing to do is make the necessary adjustments and try to live with them as best as you can.

If the roof is leaking and you cannot avoid the rain, just patch it up. If you have a lot of household chores but taking care of your baby makes juggling of tasks almost impossible, simply leave some tasks for the next day. If working with your colleagues is tense, learn to adapt to their attitude to create a civil, if not amicable, relationship.

Adaptation means you have to blend in and adjust your standards to accept others. You have to be open to compromises if they are for the best. You do not have to forsake your own principles, but you have to be open to different ways if you want to live a harmonious life with the stressful world around you.

Once you have taken these steps, relaxation naturally follows. To make it even more helpful, you have to consciously adopt a relaxing way of living and practice different relaxation techniques.

In the following chapters, you learn many tips about living an emotionally, mentally, and physically fulfilling life, as well as how to induce relaxation techniques that you turn into habits. Many of these techniques are meant to program the sensation and memory of relaxation to your system, so your mind and body can naturally fight off stress and its complications.

In the simplest sense, balancing stress and relaxation means being conscious about their levels to determine if you have too much of either one.

That means that too much relaxation without stress is also bad.

Achieving the highest form of relaxation is said to be equivalent to achieving the highest form of inner peace. However, too much relaxation is unhealthy because you might start taking things for granted, including work and relationships. For a fact, conflicts and pressure bring out the best in people, so without them, your life might fall into a rut.

Marital conflict, when properly managed, can result in a harmonious relationship because you learn more about each other, including strengths and weaknesses.

Ignoring a deadline might reduce your worries, but it lowers the quality of your work since you failed to meet the deadline. Some people even think better when they near a deadline, such as students who study at the last minute.

No one can deny that feeling some stress allows you to grow by learning more about yourself – your capabilities, strengths and weaknesses, and emotions. You have to acknowledge the function of stress in your life and in the society to truly accept and manage it. Remember that this is not about eliminating stress completely but, rather, learning how to reduce and properly manage it by balancing it with relaxation.

Chapter 2: Identifying Common Stressors

To effectively manage stress, it is natural to pinpoint the causes first – the stressors! They can be people, tangible things, real events and situations, complicated circumstances, threats, and of course, your own mental state. The mind has a huge imagination that, most of the time, creates problems even when there are none.

Because society is fast-paced, you sometimes overlook stressors, mistaking them for things you are obliged to adapt to even when avoiding them is possible.

For instance, your workplace is probably so toxic that you already accepted it as the reality, even though you can still do something about it to improve the situation. That is not called stress management but mere tolerance. However, stress simply builds inside you because some stressors just keep coming no matter how well you dodge others For example, your utility bills keep on coming every month, unfortunately.

Thus, you have to identify the common stressors in your daily life.

Urgency. The urgency of a matter prompts people to act hastily, sometimes recklessly. It results in confusion, mistakes, impatience, and indecisiveness, which brings more emotional stress. Rushing is stressful as it increases stress hormone level called cortisol, which further stirs up your emotions.

Lack of time. When you get closer to a deadline, you tend to lose confidence and start to doubt yourself. Soon after, negative emotions rush in and stress manifests as anxiety. Focus and sound judgment can be compromised, but you still do not pay much attention because time is a more pressing matter than your feelings and preferences.

Bad attitude. When you encounter a person with bad attitude, you start to feel conflict between you and the other person. The stress you feel stems from the desire to change the person and have them follow your standards. It can also pertain to your own attitude if you often treat yourself harshly for even the smallest mistakes.

Anger. Extreme stress can lead to anger, but anger alone can breed numerous negative emotions and trigger more stress. Anger makes any task harder, and emotional control becomes challenging. Thus, everything becomes more stressful even when it should not be in the first place. A simple task done with anger can become a major source of stress.

Overwhelming tasks. Taking on too many leads to exhaustion and poorly thought out decisions. This is the result of wanting to impress by working hard or the lack of analytical skill to properly assess situations. At the point where the completion of tasks no longer seems possible, your mind and body stop functioning at their best since there seems to be no point after all.

Clutter. Organization allows the mind to comprehend the task at hand, and because you think you see the whole picture, it gives you the impression that you can control it. Whenever you feel in control, stress becomes less of an issue.

However, when you see clutter or even feel it, the sense of control disappears. Studies have confirmed that people who live in a cluttered house tend to have more problems with their relationships, and employees who constantly have cluttered desks become less efficient at work.

Threat. Any kind of threat brings mental and emotional instability, and scientifically speaking, any sense of danger automatically increases cortisol production to activate your flight-or-fight mode.

Insecurity. Peace of mind is always linked to a sense of security. Without it, doubts seep in, and uncertainty is definitely something to worry about.

Exhaustion. The lack of rest and recreation leads to physical, mental, and emotional exhaustion, which leads to constant stress. You have to learn to take care of yourself if you want to feel good all the time.

Loneliness. The lack of human interaction is like keeping yourself in the dark. You might not notice the changes in your behavior and mentality, but loneliness breeds insecurity, and insecurity breeds stress and fear.

Unhealthy habits. Not eating at the right time, lack of sleep, smoking, and heavy drinking all cause physical stress that triggers the body's cortisol production. As a result, you become emotionally unstable and less focused.

Over-expectation. Whenever you set a very high expectation for an outcome, the level of disappointment upon failing to achieve your expectation also becomes bigger. Thus, the stress level is aggravated even for the smallest things.

Unfortunately, over-expectation is also one of the most common stressors that could be easily avoided.

Deprivation. Physical and emotional deprivations make the mind and body want something more. At the same time, you become more stressed because you will not give yourself what you really need.

Trauma. Traumatic experiences first cause stress, but later on without help and support, they can cause real mental disorders, including posttraumatic stress disorder (PTSD) and phobias.

Heartbreak. Heartbreak can refer to two things: frustration and lack of reciprocity. You can get frustrated for not receiving attention from someone you love, and this is self-imposed stress. You can also lack reciprocity when in a relationship, and the stress comes from insecurity and fear. Either way, you have the choice to move on and end the stress once and for all.

Death of a loved one. The death of a loved one is a natural source of short-term stress. However, if it extends to several months or years without apparent changes in symptoms, it might be a case of clinical depression or PTSD, which brings constant stress.

Poor diet. The body needs proper nutrition to counter the effects of stress and the production of too much stress hormone. Your body has to be physically fit for the mind to function efficiently.

Financial problem. Seven out of 10 Americans say their main source of stress is financial problems. Everyone feels it at some point anyway, but if stress is not vented out, it can lead to clinical depression as concluded in a study published in the *American Journal of Epidemiology.*

Physical inactivity. A sedentary lifestyle increases cortisol level and decreases the production of feel-good hormones called dopamine and serotonin, which makes matters even worse.

Pain. The mind feels what the body feels. More so, the mind can even exaggerate mild pain because of fear, making it even more stressful.

Chapter 3: Defining Stress In The Mind

Many times, the source of stress is not real but just a mere figment of the imagination. Poor mentality and ineffective coping mechanisms becomes a regular part of your system over time. Afterward, you fail to notice how they are taking over your natural responses and decisions. As you make them a habit, the mind starts to automatically create stressful thoughts and actions when you are put under pressure. These are not necessarily your desires or chosen responses but because your mind thinks that way automatically, you let the response take over without pondering the circumstances.

Have you ever noticed that you start to become stressed even just hearing someone like your boss start to speak, or upon seeing something, like a hospital? Many students start to feel distressed once the teacher of their most hated subject enters the room, while some employees feel mentally tired even before they get to work because they already know what to expect.

These are stress programs: stresses that are embedded in the mind because of past experiences, expectations, and fears. They do not necessarily exist, but a single incident in the past can lead to future assumptions because your mind adopts it as the truth. Unfortunately, you cannot achieve real relaxation without deleting these programs in your mind first.

What are the mindsets that create your stress programs?

Perfectionism. When you set high standard in everything, you also give yourself more room for disappointments and frustrations. The process of achieving the expectations you set is already long and tedious, but the failure after not achieving them is even more debilitating.

There is nothing wrong with setting high standards because it is a part personal improvement. However, when these standards become unrealistic, you tend to lose hold of the truth by burying yourself in unattainable aspirations. You continue to lose logical reasoning until you adopt impossibility as the new reality.

Perfectionism often starts from the desire to impress, stand out, and prove one's worth. However, do you really have to be perfect to gain acknowledgment?

People who believe in perfectionism have a notion that they can only be accepted and recognized if they keep that standard all the time. They fear that they are defined by their perfection and that people will take them as worthless if they do not maintain perfection.

However, in reality, people only care if you do right or wrong. You will not be constantly questioned for your mistakes. Rather, you will be questioned for not showing resiliency and admission of your mistakes.

Before you impose a perfection rule upon yourself, ask first if it is attainable to begin with. Is it necessary? Remember that perfection is sometimes boring, and trying to achieve this takes away your opportunity to learn even more and prove that you are capable of bouncing back after every fall. If you think about it, success after failure is more inspiring than holding yourself to a level of perfection that few people can relate to.

Enviousness. Another source of frustration and disappointment is enviousness. When you envy other people, you emphasize your imperfections. You treat yourself harshly for not being the best, and that only adds to your stress and self-pity.

Usually, you want to achieve and possess something that others have without considering your own abilities. Eventually, you end up losing simply because you fail to take into consideration everything you have, and instead, you look at others as if they are the golden standards. You forget your own good qualities.

Wanting to be like someone better than you is natural because it shows your desire to improve. However, when you start to become obsessed in a self-imposed competition that only you participate in, you start a vicious cycle of losing because as the only contestant, you create unnecessary stress for yourself. The frustrations and disappointments go in an endless circle, giving you something to worry about even when there is nothing there.

Instead of focusing on other people's qualities, focus on yourself first to find your strengths and weaknesses. You might be surprised that your special quality is something that other people are also admiring.

Procrastination. Habitually delaying inevitable responsibilities is pointless because you still have to do them at some point. Procrastinators argue that delaying allows time to consider their options and rethink their plans. However, most do not practice this.

Procrastination can be the result of perfectionism and low self-esteem. However, delaying does not make things better or solve your problems. You may think that delaying gives you additional time and pushes back deadlines, but the truth is, nothing changes except for your time to work, which is now shorter.

In the end, you unnecessarily put yourself under pressure, which also endangers the quality of your work. Although you feel false comfort with the free time, you will eventually suffer bigger consequences because you give yourself less time to produce good work.

Next time you procrastinate, ask yourself these questions first:

"Does it make the task easier?"

"Will it really extend your time?"

"Will you be able to achieve perfection if you wait a little longer?"

If you think procrastination does not change anything, it is far better to finish earlier and have some time to relax in the end.

Self-doubting. This shows low self-esteem. The lack of faith in your own abilities adds more pressure to your tasks because you create more things to worry about, like other people's opinions and your reputation. Maybe you have experienced failures in the past or have heard other people throw insults at you, but you are stronger than that.

Life is not about mistakes and handicaps but about redemption and resiliency. You are not judged by what you cannot do but, rather, by what you choose to not do. Continuing to doubt yourself only proves other people's opinions about you. Worse, doubting yourself all the time adds stress to your life because it makes challenges even bigger.

It is a mystery why many people opt to consciously doubt themselves. Is there satisfaction in it? Do you get a prize for being consistent with your self-doubting? Does it make you rich? If not, what is stopping you from believing in yourself?

You will probably say that fear is stopping you from appreciating yourself. You fear you are bound to fail over and over again – that people will see you as failure no matter what you do.

The stress you get from creating ghosts will never go away unless you start to feel good about yourself in your own skin.

Pessimism. When you believe that everything will always go wrong at some point, you are really likely to commit mistakes – not because you are right but because your body tends to follow what your mind feeds it. Looking forward to the unknown can give you either peace of mind or emotional torture. It is a matter of choice.

When answers are yet to be given, like the result of your action or the outcome of an event, you can choose to take the waiting time to relax or worry some more. Since both options do not yield guarantee, there is no reason to choose to worry. By relaxing instead, you also choose to care for yourself mentally, emotionally, and physically.

Keeping negativity close makes it impossible to relax. It is like a dirty secret that constantly scares you even if you really have nothing to hide. Negativity affects you to a point where you no longer believe even in the power of relaxation, and that positive thinking takes you nowhere because everything will fall apart soon enough anyway, in your mind. It creates endless worries that unnecessarily put you through mental and emotional torture.

Keeping a negative mentality does not solve anything. It has no function in your life. Instead of attracting bad vibes, lighten up your mood by thinking of beautiful things when your thoughts start to become dark. If you are feeling hopeless, close your eyes for a minute, and imagine the best-case scenario, or better yet, the best outcome you ever wanted.

Chapter 4: Battling Stress At Work

Do you know that the workplace is a bigger source of stress than your own home? Everything is potentially stressful: attendance, salary, performance rating, professional relationships, and reputation.

Before you break down from the pressure of the cutthroat industry you are in, follow these stress-busting tips first and enjoy the great career ahead of you.

1. Take your coffee break with a group

Hold your breath, but you are in for a surprise. The University of Bristol in England reported that people who consume caffeinated drinks regularly have a higher stress level. However, people who consume caffeinated drinks regularly with friends and colleagues actually showed less signs of stress. Researchers are still baffled, but the consistency of data shows strong evidence that coffee matched with a hearty conversation leads to mood enhancement. Coffee is, after all, a rich source of antioxidants.

2. Eat small portions at work

Work plus too much food equals stress. When you overeat, you also lower the ghrelin production in your body. This is a feel-good hormone that is only secreted when you are hungry. If you always keep your stomach full and your work starts to bombard you with stress, it will result in lower mental efficiency and an emotional imbalance.

Have you ever noticed how you feel sleepy or lazy after a large meal? Hunger is a natural function of the body that signals a lot of activity. If you keep hunger from occurring, your body might not handle physical and emotional stress properly.

3. Say sorry

Many people do not say "sorry" a lot at work because pride is at stake. Even when you take accountability, the tendency is to promise a solution but not show regret. Take note, though, that your own pride is one of the primary sources of stress at work.

According to Dr. Charles Emery of the Ohio State University, admitting mistakes and expressing apologies lowers your stress level because it clears the atmosphere and reduces subconscious worries that can develop into fear. Expressing regret at the right time and in the right way lightens your emotional load.

4. Take a breather

When the workday moves fast, take time to slow down to relax your tired mind and body. A minute of pause does not take away too much from your output, and in fact, it improves your productivity and quality of work.

Close your eyes and take a deep breath. Relax your back and shoulders while massaging your hands or temples. You can also store a stress ball in your drawer to relieve the tension you feel.

If your eyes have been in front of the computer for too long already, look in the distance or just look up for a minute. Look for plain surfaces, such as wall, ceiling, or floor. It is also advisable that you keep anything green, blue, brown, or orange nearby where you can focus your eyes for a minute should you feel confused and exhausted at any point.

Taking a break at work not only reduces stress but reduces the risk of carpal-tunnel syndrome and chronic back pain.

5. Have a change of environment

There is a reason why vacation leaves exist, says Dr. Srini Pillay, the head of the Panic Disorder Research Program at the McLean Hospital in Massachusetts. Changing from your stressful workplace to a relaxing environment at least once a year is like a reset button that cleans up your internal memory from damaged programs. It reminds you of positive emotions you probably no longer feel at work, such as elation, excitement, assurance, and passion.

Many companies now offer mandatory vacation leave credits not because they want their employees to go away but because they know that de-stressing is crucial for top performance. It does not matter if you choose to go to a cruise to the Caribbean or a take time off near your home. Just go out, enjoy, and forget about work for a while.

6. Make a schedule

Do not let your day be dictated by what lands first on your desk. You need to have a routine based on prioritization, so you can work steadily through the day.

Handle the most urgent tasks before proceeding with other matters. It will also help to group your tasks to make things organized. It is ideal to start with answering emails or returning phone calls. You should also stick with your breaks, so your internal program can remember relaxation during lunch and coffee breaks. That means you have to avoid working through your break, unless it is urgent. Instead of working on your resting time, it is better to render overtime.

7. Set realistic goals

When you enter a profession, you often look forward to the highest reward, like a salary increase or promotion. Most bartenders look forward to having their own bar someday. Most entry-level staff dreams of becoming executives. Goals keep employees going, but sometimes, they tend to set unrealistic goals that make their work even more stressful than it already is.

Before questioning your worth and abilities, ask yourself objective questions first.

Do your experience and educational accomplishments qualify you for the position you want to get?

Is your tenure enough for a promotion or salary increase?

How many successes and failures do you have to back up your candidacy for a promotion?

Do other employees also have impressive records and great personalities?

You have to weigh your chances based on the available considerations and not on your own desires.

Chapter 5: Practicing Relaxation Techniques

Sometimes, relaxation does not come to you unless you call for it. To help you find the inner peace to help control your stress, here are some of the most effective relaxation techniques you can try anywhere.

Bhramari Pranayam

Humming while exhaling brings a different kind of relaxation, which is usually practiced under Bhramari Pranayam, a type of meditative yoga that incorporates breathing exercises and physical relaxation.

While in a relaxed position, close your eyes and focus your mind on your breathing and not on any distractions. Plug your ears with your index fingers, then, let the air out of your chest slowly while vibrating your throat with a humming sound. Experts consider this kind of breathing exercise a form of self-hypnosis and meditation combined.

Yoga Nidra

Also called yogi sleep, this technique is said to put a person into one of the highest forms of deep relaxation by the process of lucid sleeping. Without physically sleeping, the mind is separated from the actual environment to induce an internal awareness rather than an awareness of the outside world.

While meditating, the mind is induced into lucid dreaming or spontaneous visualization to calm the body. As experts on yoga nidra put it, it is practically going into a sleep state with the conscious mind open.

Self-hypnosis

This is a procedure commonly performed under modern hypnotherapy. It has four stages – motivation, relaxation, concentration, and directing.

In the first stage, a person has to find his motivation – the biggest reason to relieve his symptoms. It can be his family, God, money or his own self. In the second stage, physical relaxation should be attained – the body and environment – anything to shutdown your senses for a while. In the third stage, you take away all thoughts and just leave a blank picture in your head. In the last stage, you have to put all your energy on visualizing a desired goal and end-result.

It is like having a peek into the future to inspire you to attain something. The goal of this procedure is to temporarily let you forget the present and focus on the future.

According to a study at Ohio State University, self-hypnosis can also enhance the immune system and solve stress, anxiety, sleep disorders, and asthma, as well.

Mind-body Relaxation

This technique aims to calm the senses to reverse the overwhelming emotions by releasing tensions that can disrupt the natural hormone production in the body. These tensions can also prematurely age a person's DNA as seen in one study at the University of California at San Francisco.

Also called the mindfulness technique and mindful meditation, it unites the mind and body by relaxing the body and letting the mind follow. In a study published at the *American Heart Association*, this technique can lower blood pressure, which is associated with anger and hot tempers. This can also relieve the signs of anxiety attack, like shaking, sweating, difficulty in breathing, and increased pulse rate.

Find a quiet place and sit down. Calm your body and senses by sitting still and not thinking of anything. Find a "point of focus" or a mental image that elicits positive emotions. Tap your memory to find events that make you smile and laugh. Make visualizations of your aspirations and goals.

Scientifically speaking, this practice aims to trigger your body to produce endorphins and lower cortisol, while normalizing the flow of your sympathetic nervous system.

Autogenic Training

Developed in the 1930s, this technique aims to program your autonomic nervous system to purge out stress regularly and physically adapt to stress symptoms biologically. It also restores the natural balance of the sympathetic nervous, which is disrupted by high stress levels.

To perform this technique, start your day with 15 minutes of meditation, visualization accompanied by a comfortable position, and deep breathing. As the term "auto" implies, you are creating a state of relaxation in your body to enable it to naturally fight stress symptoms the next time they arise. For this to succeed, it is important to do it every day.

Decompression

According to a specialist from the Ohio State University Wexner Medical Center located in Columbus, this is an effective way of releasing the accumulated tension from the body and relaxing aching muscles and joints. To do this, get a warm bag or heat wrap and apply it to your neck and shoulder for at least 10 minutes. Do it as well on body parts that are starting to feel aches and sores.

End this relaxation technique by applying pressure using a ball or massage roller. Place a ball (the size of a basketball) between your back and the wall. Gently move your back on all directions so the ball presses onto your back. Massage your shoulders, legs, and arms with a roller by slowly rolling it over the areas.

Bodyscan Meditation

In this relaxation technique, the mind and body is realigned with the senses. To do this, lie down with straight body, free of movement, and relax until your body is free of tensions and your mind is undistracted. Now, start with subtle movements from your toes, to your feet, then up to your core then to your arms and head. Picture a scanning process on your body to check if anything is wrong.

As you gently move your body parts one by one, feel all the sensations while being consistent with your deep breathing. Now, visualize the air flowing through your nose down to your lungs, then to other body parts. It is important to inhale through your nose and exhale through your mouth.

Sensual Visualization

This is a type of meditation that tries to integrate all the senses in visualizing. If you feel stressed out and you have 10 minutes of free time, use it to place yourself under a trance that mimics all the relaxing sensations of your body.

To do this, close your eyes and relax your body while breathing deeply yet slowly. Now, instead of just thinking about beautiful and inspiring pictures in your head, imagine the sensations being relaxed.

Try to recreate the feeling of fresh green grass under your feet, or the gentle breeze from the ocean kissing your face. Imagine your loved one hugging you, and feel the warmth of the embrace.

Recall what you felt the last time you smelled lavender or jasmine or when you walked in a garden full of blooming flowers and lush greeneries.

Think of your ultimate comfort food, and imagine yourself taking a bite of that mouthwatering peace of heaven. Imagine the most scrumptious cake you have ever had, and recall what it tasted like as you melt the crumbs inside your mouth. Maybe a sip of sparkling champagne also reminds you the ambience of the coziest restaurant you ever dined in.

You can also think about things that remind you of the happiest moments of your life. Think of your dog as you play with it. Visualize the atmosphere in your first romantic date. Or, listen to the most romantic song you have ever heard in your head. Melodies do not fade in the mind, and maybe you can even sing along.

Body shaking

Physical symptoms appear when cortisol level rises in the body, says Massachusetts-based sports psychologist Dr. Alan Goldberg. This is the same reason why metabolism slows down, muscles shrink faster, and joints become stiffer when a person is distressed.

You can stop your stress hormone from rising by simply shaking off your stress like how you would when warming up for an exercise. Shake off the stress from your hands and feet, then the joints down to your muscle groups. Loosening up your muscles and joints relaxes them and fights the physical effects of stress in your body.

Smile

Yes, smiling is a simple yet effective relaxation technique. Smiling does a lot more than reduce stress in the body but also extends your lifespan by several years. This simple facial expression is enough to boost your production of endorphins, potent feel-good hormones. It does not even matter if your smile is genuine or not because experts found out that when you smile a lot, the good mood comes next whether you like it or not.

Magic Mirror Technique

It is not a magic spell, but it might magically make your stress disappear in a matter of minutes. This technique follows the principle of reflexology where the tips of the fingers affect mood and pain in the head.

All you have to do is press the fingers in your left hand against the fingers in your right hand like how you do it when placing your hand on a mirror. Put pressure on both hands, and then start to push against each other before releasing. Do it in quick successions. If you close your eyes, you will feel like you are pressing against a mirror; thus, the name.

Sauna Bath

If you have a little more time to visit a spa or sauna house, a sauna bath will not only detoxify you physically but also mentally and emotionally. According to a study conducted at Oklahoma State University, people who take sauna baths have a greater sense of accomplishment, can relax faster, and ward off stress easier compared to people who do counseling alone. This is also a perfect way to end a heavy workout session.

Balancing

You will need an exercise ball for this technique. All you have to do is sit on top, feet up, and balance for a few minutes. It is an effective workout to strengthen your core, but the real point of this technique is to restore your sense of balance. This will help if you feel like your feet are always moving fast on the ground or if your head is floating from so much work.

Practice this everyday, and you will feel the difference.

Ear Massage

Press your earlobes in soft, circular motions using your thumb and index fingers. Do this for 15 seconds before releasing. This ear massage stimulates your tentorium membrane, which has direct effect to your stress level. It makes you more relaxed and emotionally stable, as shown in a study done by the Muscular Therapy Center in New York City.

Chapter 6: Managing Stress At Home

De-stressing in a luxurious spa with your personal masseuse is probably your idea of relaxation. Many people also travel halfway around the globe in search for the most breathtaking paradise, and the magnificent view in itself is what they call relaxation. There are a lot of ways to beat stress and induce relaxation by spending your hard-earned money. However, you can successfully achieve inner peace right in the comforts of your home – with no additional charges.

Here are some effective ways to manage stress at home.

1. Make orange juice your new coffee

Orange juice is the ideal stress buster because of two things: it is high in vitamin C, and it contains certain polyphenols that stimulate the production of oxytocin, a feel-good hormone. A study conducted at the University of Alabama found that 200 milligrams of vitamin C from natural food sources is enough to lower the secretion of cortisol.

2. Stock some dark chocolates

Dark chocolates are some of the most effective natural stress relievers. Who does not love chocolates? However, more than their addicting bitter-sweetness is their power to enhance your positive mood by lowering the secretion of cortisol. They are also rich in a compound called phenylethylamine that can stimulate the brain to produce another hormone that emulates the feeling of being in love. Now you know why chocolate is a fast way to get someone fall in love with you.

3. Load yourself with green tea antioxidants

Green tea has more caffeine than your regular coffee. That makes it potentially harmful for already stressed out people. However, when taken in moderate, controlled amounts, in addition to a dose of cancer-fighting chemical compounds, it can be a friend more than a foe. In this case, the benefit of green tea actually outweighs its possible side effects.

A single cup of green tea has overwhelming theanine content, a type of amino acid that not only fights carcinogens but also considerably boosts mental performance. It supports mental clarity, which is very important in straightening out thoughts during stressful times.

4. Make organic beef your source of protein

Organic foods are now becoming the standard for alternative healing, whether it is for a dreaded disease or for stress. There is a school of thought that points to processed foods and additives as one of the primary reasons for the prevalence and occurrence of new dreaded diseases, from the rapid increase of cancer cases to the worsening of mental disorders. Thus, going back to organic and natural foods solves all health conditions created by poor eating habits.

Organic beef has more antioxidants – beta-carotene, coenzyme Q10, vitamin C and vitamin E – than any meat because it has never been altered by drugs, antibiotics and hormones. That means you get the defense you need against the symptoms of stress without the risk of having cumulative side effects in the future.

The *British Journal of Nutrition* also published a study where researchers discovered that eating organic beef increases omega-3 fatty acid in the blood while decreasing omega-6 fatty acid, which is linked to higher rate of inflammatory conditions. These changes in the body are connected to lower risk of stress and depression.

5. Play with a dog

You can trade a masseuse for a dog and still end up de-stressed. Researchers from the State University of New York at Buffalo discovered that people who regularly play with dogs record lower cortisol level in the body and lower risk of cardiovascular diseases. There is really no need to back up the claim with a study since everybody seems to know this.

6. Listen to instrumental and classical music

Start your day with music or finish the household chores while listening to instrumental and classical melodies. Music is a very effective therapy that not only beats stress but also boosts the immune system and lowers the risk of catching the common cold, researchers from the Wilkes University in Pennsylvania reported.

If you are not into bland music, the best alternatives are Enya and the diva herself, Celine Dion. Her powerful voice is said to be the most effective stress reliever among all contemporary singers.

7. Hug

Where else can you make hugging a habit but at home with your family? Hug therapy is now becoming a modern take on alternative healing, and although it seems absurd, it is really backed up by a scientific study.

According to researchers from University of North Carolina, hugging is as effective as sex when it comes to beating stress. It enhances mood and boosts energy quickly. Researchers found out that habitual hugging increases oxytocin, a hormone that lightens up the mood, decreases cortisol, and improves blood pressure.

Similar benefits were also seen in other physical contacts, such as holding hands, cuddling, and tickling. Incorporating physical contact in showing your affection is said to permanently reduce mood swings.

In a separate study at the same university, researchers found out that merely holding your lover's hand for 10 minutes lowers blood pressure and stabilizes heart rate even when under stress.

8. Stretch every morning

Stretching does more than revitalize your energy, improve blood circulation, and stimulate metabolism. It is also a good way to jumpstart your mood as it boosts endorphin production. Endorphins are another feel-good hormone that not only stabilizes emotion but also acts as natural pain reliever to help you ward off the physical symptoms of stress.

Start your day with five to 15 minutes of stretching, from the head downwards. You can also proceed with 30 minutes of cardio exercises. However, avoid resistance and strength training this early because physical stress can also stimulate cortisol production.

9. Have sex

This is not to encourage you to make sex the center of your de-stressing rituals. Rather, it is a reminder that you can never underestimate the power of an explosive orgasm in releasing your emotional and mental stress.

Sex and masturbation lower cortisol by boosting your beta-endorphin, the body's natural pain reliever. That means you become tougher against the symptoms of stress and your emotions become harder to dampen. Also, a survey shows that people who have an active sex life are happier than others.

10. Make pasta a Sunday meal

In a study published in *Alcoholism: Clinical and Experimental Research,* experts found that the complex carbohydrates found in pasta is enough to boost the brain's serotonin level by 100 percent. It prevents anxiety, panic attacks, depression, and aggression by inducing relaxation. Add a little organic beef and you get the best natural anti-depressant.

11. Have a hobby

Hobbies give you an output for stored energy, which is sometimes overflowing when you are under too much stress. Instead of using that energy to vent out anger, focus instead on other physical activities you find exciting and relaxing. The author of *Stress Management Made Simple*, Dr. Jay Winner, emphasizes that mental and emotional energy, when not converted to physical energy, become harmful and aggressive.

12. Iron clothes

Dr. Winner adds that if there is one household chore you can call the most de-stressing, it is ironing. The repetitive hand motion of ironing while looking at straightened lines put you under a trance that clears your mind from distressing thoughts. It is the best way to end your overwhelming household chores.

Conclusion

I hope this book was able to help you understand more about your stress and the different ways to get it under control.

The next step is to clear your mind and believe that stress is not more powerful than you. Find the relaxation technique that best works for you, and find other things that make you feel good. De-stressing is a life-long process, so you should not stop looking for excitement and happiness. Remember that your mind controls your body, and whatever you put in it is reflected physically.

Thank you and good luck!